I050440ɓ

# Ethereum

## Unlock the Secret World of Ethereum

Ethereum Wallet, Ethereum Mining, Ethereum
Investing and Trading, Smart Contracts, ERC-20,
Dapps, Proof of Stake (PoS), ETH, Blockchain 2.0

New Edition

By Kerry Gan

# Disclaimer

All information and data in this book is for informational purpose only. I make no representations as to the accuracy, completeness, suitability, or validity of any information. I will not be liable for any errors, omissions, or any losses, injuries, or damages arising from its display or use.

Because the information in this book is based on my personal opinion and experience, it should not consider professional financial investment advice. The ideas and strategies should never be used without first assessing your own personal and financial situation, or without consulting a financial professional.

My thoughts and opinions will also change from time to time as I learn and accumulate more knowledge. In any event, I'm not providing any Services (including but not limited to advisory services) relating to any securities in any jurisdiction.

# Table of Contents

# Introduction

Although Ethereum is the second-largest cryptocurrency and has a market cap of about $69 billion, not everyone is aware of the technology behind it, or the issues that it seeks to solve.

To worsen matters, some people are entirely ignorant of its existence. A survey carried out by a well-established financial body reported that only 25% of its over 1000 respondents were aware of Ethereum.

This book seeks to simplify the Ethereum concept and demystify what would usually be perceived as "technical" or "complex." After going through the content of this book, readers will have an in-depth understanding of Ethereum and can finally make informed decisions about the cryptocurrency.

# What is Ethereum, and why people called it Blockchain 2.0?

Ethereum is an open-source, blockchain-based distributed computing platform and operating system which features the smart contract functionality.

It supports a modified version of the Nakamoto (Bitcoin) consensus through transaction-based state transitions.

Ethereum enables smart contracts and distributed applications (DApps) to be developed and used without any interruption, scam, control, or interference from a third party. (This might have given Ethereum its alias 'Blockchain 2.0')

Ethereum is suited for building economic systems in pure software. In other words, the software is for commercial logic, where users can move money around with the speed and scale that can be gotten with data as opposed to the 3-7-day floating period that applies to the commercial banking system, or the fees associated with already established vendors.

With a simple Ethereum application, for example, it is quite easy to pay a whole lot of people, in different locations around the world, and in small amounts every few minutes, while in the conventional banking system people would have to use an entire payroll department working round the clock to continually reconcile their account books and deal with the cross-border issues.

Ethereum is more than just a blockchain; it is a distributed programmable blockchain-based software platform. In a way, it can be reported that Ethereum is tied to its cryptocurrency token (Ether – ETH), which runs the Ethereum network.

A very prominent feature of Ethereum is the smart contract. A smart contract is a computer code that can aid the exchange of cash, content, assets, stocks, or anything of value.

A smart contract runs on the blockchain network and functions as a self-operating computer program, which is automatically executed when precise conditions are met.

Although all blockchains can process code, quite a lot are really limited. Ethereum, however, is different. Instead of limiting developers, Ethereum allows developers to create whatever operations they want.

This implies that developers can build various applications that can surpass anything that can be imagined.

The integral programming language-Solidity- is used to write smart contracts and DApps. Subsequently, the cryptocurrency asset (Ether) helps in implementing these apps and contracts.

Therefore, Ethereum is also referred to as programmable money. It is important to note that the idea of Ethereum was not just creating another cryptocurrency with similar characteristics with Bitcoin.

Instead, it was created based on the need to code, run, and execute smart contracts and DApps autonomously without the need for human interference.

Ethereum was primarily described in a white paper by Vitalik Buterin, a young developer who was involved with bitcoin magazine in the concluding part of 2013.

Ethereum was officially introduced with a surprisingly long list of founders (considering that Bitcoin was published anonymously), which served to give it more credence to its potential users.

When Dr. Gavin Wood became a part of the Ethereum team, the Ethereum Foundation funded the advancement of Ethereum software, and about $18 million was crowdsourced in the of Ether tokens before they were officially available.

Anyone with a computer or smartphone can try the platform out if they own 'ether'-unique pieces of code that allow updates to the blockchains ledger.

Ethereum wallet helps secure a place to securely store ether or at least a place to store your private keys.

One caveat is that losing a unique private key is much bigger a deal than misplacing a password; it means losing ether, forever.

Removing trusted parties is a two-edged sword. While intermediaries are no longer needed to verify the transaction, there is no help desk to turn to for help to recover any lost secret key.

It may appear that the wallet and exchange lingo up to this point has been quite like bitcoin. However, the application of Ethereum is quite different.

Ethereum has an admittedly confusing storage system. In this system, there are two primary components that users need for identification; the public key and the private key.

Usually represented as a scrambled string of letters and numbers, the two keys are linked together by cryptography.

Safety of financial data and other significant information has been a primary worldwide concern to big players in the tech industry and even those who just started in the industry.

Interestingly, there has been an extensive adoption of this technology to advance security in times past as part of attempts to reinforce prevailing security solutions.

Nowadays, several developers and blockchain companies are interested in using the Ethereum platform to build and design a range of applications.

# Dark history of Ethereum

## The Dao hack

One of the most mind-blowing ideas to be effectively executed by blockchain technology is the Decentralized autonomous organization (DAO).

Decentralized autonomous organizations are bodies that function using smart contracts.

The Ethereum platform allowes developers who had ideas would propose their concept to the crypto community and possibly obtain funding from the decentralized autonomous organizations.

With the way it was structured, users who possessed the DAO tokens could elect proposed ideas and in turn, would earn bonuses if the ideas turned out to be profitable.

Unfortunately, on the 17th of June 2016, a glitch in the DAO codes was found by a hacker, enabling him to empty funds from the DAO.

This resulted in a loss of about 3.6 million ETH (almost 70 million USD at that time). As soon as the hacker got the money out of the system, he restored the system.

In this hack, the attacker was able to make a request from the DAO smart contract to pay out ether several times before what was left of the smart contract could be updated.

After the attack, it was speculated that the fact that the coders of the DAO smart did not take into cognizance the likelihood of a recursive call and that the internal token balance was updated after the ETH funds were transferred were reasons for this hack.

It's vital to recognize that this issue did not directly emanate from Ethereum itself, but from the DAO that was built on Ethereum.

## Crypto kitty traffic jam

Yet another negative story that was linked to Ethereum was the unusually slow network caused because of Cryptokitties, a game built on the Ethereum blockchain where players spend ether to breed cartoon kittens or trade with other players.

It was recorded that the collectors of the digital tchotchkes clogged up the Ethereum network, suspending transactions, and triggering a collision of untreated transactions.

Unprocessed Ethereum transactions rose about six-fold since the release of CryptoKitties was released, with the game having the most engaged address on the Ethereum network, which was responsible for nearly 12% of all transactions.

## Collapse of ICO

When they were first introduced (chiefly based on the Ethereum platform), Initial Coin Offerings (ICOs) presented tokens for everybody and every function.

However, in the middle of 2018, things started to look a lot different for both existing tokens and initial coin offerings.

There was a drastic reduction in the number of ICOs that were attempting to raise funding.

This was caused by numerous factors, among which were vagueness around regulation, deteriorating crypto market prices and, the disappointment in the preceding ICOs that raised capital.

Owing to the fact that the Ethereum blockchain was the leading platform for ICOs to raise their funding, it bore the brunt of the drastic reduction in the amount of ICOs seeking funding.

Subsequently, this caused adverse effects on the price of ETH, but also caused existing ICOs to convert their ETH into Fiat currency to meet costs, further driving its price lower.

# 4 Benefits of Ethereum over Bitcoin

With all the hype surrounding cryptocurrency and blockchain, many people are torn between Bitcoin and Ethereum, and it not uncommon for newbies in the crypto sphere to try to make comparisons between these two remarkable cryptocurrencies.

Even though both systems are trying to do things in their own way, there are certainly some distinguishing features between them.

The competition between Bitcoin and Ethereum has been apparent since Ethereum's launch. Over the years, Ethereum has been able to give Bitcoin a strong contest when it comes to captivating people's hearts and winning their attention.

It is even believed that some people that have had issues with bitcoin have found solace in Ethereum. Below are some ways in which Ethereum might be preferable over Bitcoin

**Speed**

Given that the block size of Bitcoin is capped at a 1 MB limit, on-chain transaction processing on the network is limited by the average block creation time of 10 minutes, now imagine a couple of thousand transactions to be carried out on this type of network!

This will result in scalability issues. Ethereum, on the other hand, can execute a more significant number of transactions without having to worry about scalability.

On average, it takes between 15 seconds and 5 minutes for an Ethereum transaction to be processed, which makes it about 20 times faster than the bitcoin transaction process, which takes longer to occur.

Ethereum has quicker block times, which makes the platform more effective. Ethereum allows for blocks, or the records of crypto-based transactions, to be generated more quickly than Bitcoin.

This efficiency ensures quicker transactions and enables Ethereum to manage the large number of transactions that take place across its network. In Ethereum, the block time is set around 15 seconds, and the network betters Bitcoin's 10-minute transaction speed through the smart handling of stale blocks by using the Ghost protocol.

**Gas**

Gas is vital to the smooth sailing of Ethereum because it makes available a technique of giving incentives that entices additional miners to the system.

Because Ethereum has been able to draw more miners, it also has a higher hash rate, which is responsible for the system being more valuable and secure.

Miners receive tokens by mining blocks, but they can also get additional tokens by provisionally governing the blocks that they mine and using them to make a profit.

When miners mine a block and encode it, computational power is also essential to authorize those contracts, and because of Ethereum's gas functionality, they can charge a fee for it, giving them another opportunity to make more money.

## Smart Contracts

Bitcoin uses blockchain technology to execute the task of sending money from one address to another.

Ethereum, on the other hand, employs its blockchain to accomplish a variety of transactions commonly referred to as smart contracts.

A smart contract is a computer code expected to implement an agreed contract digitally; they ensure the accomplishment of trustworthy transactions with no need for third-party interference.

People from various parts of the world can network and exchange value exclusive of a centralized authority when they use a smart contract.

## Application Platform

Although Bitcoin functions well as a store of value, it still has some shortcomings when it is treated as a medium of exchange.

Ethereum has the main advantage of being a technology that allows for computer applications to run on the network.

Since the Ethereum network enables smart contracts, apps, and contains the internal currency ether, there is a fast growth of the platform with several apps being built on Ethereum; the network is also used by start-ups to raise money via initial coin offerings which further increases the network's importance.

# 4 Ways to get Ethereum for Free

You might find it hard to believe that it is possible for you to get Ethereum even when you do not have enough money to invest in mining or buying it, but this is true.

There are websites in which Ethereum gives out Ethereum for free.

They are called Ethereum faucets (a faucet is like a lottery that issues a given number of altcoins in a given duration), and they offer rewards in the form of small amounts of ETH in exchange for finishing captchas or relating with several ads.

To be factual, the amount of ETH you will earn at the end of the day is quite small, even if you decide to do a lot of recurring small tasks and interact with the ads.

Most of these sites also have a minimum amount of Ether you need to earn before you can make withdrawals. Some of these sites are:

**EtherFaucetNet**

EtherFaucetNet is a faucet that affords users the

chance to receive Ethers after every 5minutes.

Users sign-in on the faucet by using their Ethereum address. As soon as this is done, they can automatically begin claiming Ethereum.

This faucet mandates users to reach a threshold of 0.05ETH, after which they can move them to their Ethereum wallet.

**Ethfree**

Ethfree is regarded as the foremost faucet which offers high amounts of Ethereum daily.

Ethfree also gives out free Ethereum tokens after every five minutes.

As was seen with the aforementioned website, users cannot transfer their earned coins until they hit the 0.05 ETH mark.

**Ethereum Gratis**

Ethereum Gratis gives Ethereum tokens to the next user online in 5 minutes intervals.

If a user is lucky to fall into this category, they get to receive 10% of the accessible Ethereum in the faucet wallet.

Nonetheless, users must attain the payable benchmark of 1fenny before they can move their earnings to their Ethereum wallet.

**Ethereum Faucet**

This Faucet entails users completing some captcha to earn Ethereum.

Also, they must sign up on the FaucetHub account before they get a chance to earn.

As soon as they get the free Ethers, their Ethereum wallets are automatically credited.

Additionally, this platform gives users the chance to receive a 10% commission for every referral that comes through them.

# ERC-20 vs ERC-721 Token

ERC (Ethereum Request for Comment) is a shared and distributed network whereby individuals in the crypto community can make and remark on bids for regulating Ethereum smart contracts and tokens.

It is important that you bear in mind that this is not in any way like the EIP (Ethereum Improvement Proposals), which affects the Ethereum practice.

ERC20 and ERC721 are common standards in the Ethereum ecosystem.

They are employed individually to signify fungible assets and non-fungible assets (respectively).

The ERC20 standard defines only the interface a smart contract and not its execution. In smart contracts, the code is ordered into valid groups called functions.

The interface of the smart contract is an account of the activities that its functions should carry out, and the execution is the real code of the functions.

The ERC721 standard was introduced by the well-liked game CryptoKitties (the same one that slowed the Ethereum traffic).

An ERC721 token individually represented the virtual kitties collected and bred by players.

While we have established that an ERC20 token epitomizes a specific type of asset, an ERC721 token denotes a group of assets.

As with CryptoKitties, the ERC721 token contract stood for all the distinctive kitties in the game, as well as who their owners are.

The ownership of the ERC721 tokens is made more straightforward; a user either wholly owns an asset or does not. For instance, it is not conceivable for a CryptoKitties user to have a partial virtual cat.

ERC-20 tokens are those that represent a value, like a currency note. They are transposable and not exclusive.

Several tokens currently available on exchanges today are ERC-20 tokens on Ethereum blockchain.

They enable the transfer of value, and they are separable. This implies that a user can give 0.001 of his tokens to another user.

While ERC-721 tokens represent an exclusive asset, comparable with a certificate of ownership for a work of art.

The ERC-721 tokens are not transposable, and even though they are valuable, the value of one token is not the same as any other token of the same type.

ERC-721 tokens are non-divisible which means users cannot give half of your token to another person.

# 5 Reasons Moving to Proof of Stake (POS)

Before we dwell on the reason for the move, it is essential to have a basic understanding of what a proof of stake is and how it works.

Proof of Stake removes all the hard work from the mining process. As a substitute for time and electricity (the means with which validators are employed in creating POW) the system allows miners with most coins (the substitute resource) to script a blockchain's history.

The fundamental value that PoS presents is that the more devoted a validator is in the network i.e., the higher their stakes in the system, the lower the probability that they would sabotage it, and consequently, they should be awarded more validating rights.

With the proof of stake system in place, a validator will only be able to mine the percentage of his investments in the system.

Therefore, below are some of the reasons why ETH made a huge switch from POW to POS.

• The cryptographic computations that will be carried out in PoS are those verifying that a miner has the required amount of crypto before he can validate.

• The subject of superfluous energy wastage will be a thing of the past, as there will be no need for traditional mining.

• There will be more volunteers for the validation process as there is no need for miners to compete for solving complex mathematical puzzles (a factor that necessitates the use of mining hardware).

• Energy costs will be drastically reduced.

• POS will make attacks on the blockchain even more expensive, discouraging potential threats.

# POS vs POW

POW is widely used in several cryptocurrency projects as it saves a lot of crypto-based applications from DDoS attacks.

Nevertheless, the extreme energy cost, amplified tension on the environment, related opposing media coverage, increasing control of mining processes, and depleted transaction quantity are factors that would make it unrealistic in the long run.

Societies are more and more worried about the high energy costs of Bitcoin mining, and this is having a negative effect on POW consensus.

On the other hand, Although POS is comparatively new, the acceptance is looking promising, for instance, the popular cryptocurrency DASH is running on this consensus.

If the proponents of POS can guarantee the extensive crypto community about the capacity of the algorithm to keep the network sufficiently, that might increase its acceptance.

If the extremely trusted Ethereum project establishes a positive transition to POS, a lot of people will pay more attention to the algorithm.

The POS procedure delivers a more accessible blockchain with higher transaction quantity.

# When Will POS Happen?

The specific date for the full implementations/transition is not yet official. Vitalik Buterin, founder of Ethereum, announced late last year that he intended to introduce a Proof of Stake (POS) this year.

The upgrade to the network is referred to as Casper. Instead of verifying transactions on the network via mining (Proof of Work), users will have the ability to 'stake' their Ether.

Although Proof of Stake is not fully executed yet, On May 8th, 2018, Ethereum released the very first version of Casper Friendly Finality Device (FFG), which is a new POS algorithm on the Github coding repository.

The release signified a massive progression towards the much-awaited transition from the existing Proof-of-Work (POW) algorithm to Proof-of-Stake (POS) algorithm.

# Top 5 Unique Decentralized Applications (Dapps)

Ethereum came up with an out-of-the-box solution when they introduced Dapps.

The Ethereum platform offers a wide selection of advanced technologies, including decentralization, smart contracts, ERC-20 tokens, proof of stake.

More than 90% of blockchain dApps (decentralized applications) are founded on Ethereum's distributed ledger, and they are expected to multiply.

Ethereum is unquestionably the ruler of smart contracts and DApps.

In case you are wondering, DApps are decentralized applications where no sole individual has the control because it is installed on a distributed ledger or the blockchain of Ethereum.

Below are some Dapps that you might find interesting and useful.

## CryptoKitties

CryptoKitties is a new Dapp that provides its users with access to virtual cats that they can purchase, trade or breed. These cats are referred to as crypto-collectibles.

The CryptoKitties app is hosted on the Ethereum blockchain. Like cryptocurrencies, the CryptoKitties app is doing well on Ethereum's blockchain.

Just like each Ether, each crypto kitty is also exclusive.

**Gnosis**

Ethereum based Gnosis is planned for forecasts, for instance, trying to find out the market prediction for a football match or a basketball match.

With Gnosis and the GNO token, users can get answers to their questions and see the prices they're interested in. Also, they can make bets and vote.

**Compound Finance**

Compound finance is the most special of DApps in 2019. They are developing a collection of apps to empower crypto loaning and borrowing.

For users that are holding on to crypto token, they can lend their cryptos to earn a substantial interest. At the same time, they can also borrow from the dApp without being compelled to do KYC and other typical paperwork.

**Etheroll**

This is perhaps the most popular Ethereum dice casino in existence.

Apart from having an exceptional 7-day transactions volume of 7,000 ETH, it also boasts of over 18,000 transactions per week.

Etheroll is an Ethereum smart contract for placing bets on a provably fair dice game using Ether with no deposits or sign-ups.

**Aragon**

Aragon is a dApp that is intended to run decentralized autonomous organizations, also known as DAOs.

With this Dapp, angel investors can access fresh and innovative ideas in the crypto sphere.

It also enhances transparency in the pitching of ideas and implementing them.

Aragon typically removes the need for third-party parties using smart contracts.

# Conclusion

As established, Ethereum is an open-source blockchain, and this implies that users can create an identification number for their transactions at any place and at any time.

Largely eliminating the need for users to wait for their bank to approve a transaction and also having to present a credit card. This essentially serves as an important advantage of Ethereum.

Ethereum is also completely protected against any third-party interventions, which implies that all the decentralized apps within the network cannot be controlled by anyone at all and has proven to be extremely resistant against attack while also sustaining a wide range of the public market.

Ethereum is designed to be low-cost, open, flexible, and suited for transactions between multiple parties. Generally, Ethereum is an open blockchain for building application has been generally accepted by users all over because of its simplicity and user-friendly abilities.

Ethereum has more to offer in addition to that.

Ethereum provides a platform to the developer on which they can build blockchain-based smart contracts and decentralized apps.

It is fascinating to see the way this technology is being resourcefully utilized across a wide range of businesses to deal with specific challenges linked with digital transactions together with currency imitations, scams, chargebacks, cross-boundary transactions, data security, and double-spending.

When it comes to usage and development, Ethereum is rapidly gaining ground with some enthusiasts asserting that it has a higher number of transactions than Bitcoin.

It is definitely not out of place to say that Ethereum will keep growing and will persist as one of the chief players on the market.

This assertion is possible for the reason that several projects that are positioned to change the face of market capitalization are deployed on Ethereum.

The continuous development of the network will ensure that there is a supportable and accessible protocol for impending global use, which is good news to the crypto community.

# Thank You

Thank you for reading! It's so amazing to see people reading my books. Like most writers, I used to think I wasn't good enough, so I didn't try. With the encouragement of my business partners, clients, friends, and family members, I was able to give this series a go. I'm eternally grateful for each reader enjoyed reading my books and put the books on their virtual shelf.

If you enjoyed this book or found it is useful, I'd be very grateful if you'd post a short review on Amazon. Your support does make a difference, and I read all the reviews personally so I can get your feedback and make the next book even better.

If you would like to explore more about cryptocurrency, make sure to check out my other crypto books on Amazon.

Once again, sincerely thank you for the support!

# About The Author

Kerry Gan is an accomplished self-published author with more than a decade of experience in Forex, Binary Option, Blockchain, and Crypto industry by holding senior positions in multiple international financial and fintech institutions.

Kerry is an early investor for Litecoin back in 2014, a private investor for EOS and IOTA. He is the Blockchain Strategist from the University of Oxford, and founding member of the Association of Blockchain Development in Hong Kong.

Kerry holds a Master of Applied Finance from the University of Adelaide, and he is also a Certified Financial Planner (CFP©) for financial planning and wealth management.